Wolf

REFLECTIONS

REFLECTIONS *of the* WILDERNESS SERIES

by

KEN L. JENKINS

Printed in Singapore
ICS BOOKS, INC.
Merrillville, Indiana

Dedication

In late fall of 1995, my young friend Jeffrey and his parents left their home in the Alaskan bush to assist a disabled vehicle along the road near Denali Park. As they approached the vehicle, one of the passengers emerged with a rifle and shot and killed Jeffery's life-long pal and lead mush dog, Teslin, because the man "thought it was a wolf." I dedicate this book to you, Jeffrey, in hopes that as you grow older, man will come to understand the delicate balance of nature, and you will learn to care and even share with those who hurt the things that we love so dearly. I'm very sorry for your loss.

Wolf Reflections

Copyright © 1996 by Ken L. Jenkins

10 9 8 7 6 5 4 3 2 1

Printed in Singapore

Published by:
ICS Books, Inc.
1370 E. 86th Place
Merrillville, IN 46410
800-541-7323

Library of Congress Cataloging-in-Publication Data

Jenkins, Ken L.
    Wolf reflections /by Ken L. Jenkins.
      p. cm. — (Reflections of the wilderness series)
    ISBN 1-57034-035-8
      1. Wolves - - North America. . 2.Wolves - - North America —pictorial works.
    I. Title. II. Series.
    QL737.C22J45 1996
    599.74'442—dc20   96-33978

Table of Contents

Acknowledgments

In trying to locate wolves, one can only listen carefully to those who live in the backcountry and then place yourself in the right habitat for extended periods of time. Many people have taken time to share wolf stories with me. Thanks to Nan Eagleson and Bob Shelton for years of friendship and lots of great information concerning their years and treks into Denali National Park, Alaska. As you mush beneath the moonlight, in the shadow of the Alaskan Range, may your dogs only stop for the song of the wolf.

Preface

Throughout my early life in the Smoky Mountains of Tennessee, I dreamed of someday exploring the Far North. My visions of dense forest, secluded mountain lakes, and untamed, rolling rivers kept me motivated to attain my goal of spending time in the "wilderness paradise" that I had formulated in my mind. As I began to develop my desire to travel to this land of unspoiled beauty, I became aware of many naturalist's writings that dealt with the very heart of my cravings. From the ramblings of John Muir to the poetry of Robert Service, and then to the naturalist's accounts by Adolph Murie, I read and reread and through their words I lived and relived the experiences. Those accounts of living with wolves and bears, braving the harsh elements, and finding romance in all of the above still inspire me today. Now, after twenty years of travel into Alaska, British Columbia, Alberta, and the Arctic regions of the Yukon and Northwest Territories, my appetite is still far from satisfied. I have felt the stinging north wind with a chill factor of minus 50. I have stood alone on Arctic islands and watched the musk oxen graze as the midnight sun touched the horizon and began to rise. I have listened to the cry of the sandhill cranes as thousands passed over my head on their sojourn south. In all of this I have found romance and beauty. There have been many unique moments that stand above the rest. Daybreak on a ridge watching a pair of wolverine hunt was surely an impressive site. Morning in the heavy mists of the Pribilof Islands with a billion sweet wildflowers scenting the air is a smell that will always be with me. I will always recall the feel of the smooth, rippled, rock slabs near Bathurst Inlet where tons of glacial ice ground and polished them not that many years ago in geological history. Above all that I have known and experienced in the northern woodlands, the first time that a pack of wolves broke the silence of a cold evening in Kootenay left a permanent impression on me. Though I heard and did not see, this revelation of the presence of the most dignified of mammals has kept me searching for the track of the wolf and the time to spend in a world that few understand. The following pages reflect on days with wolves and nature.

It seems almost something abnormal that over a portion of the earth's surface nature should be nothing and man everything.
—Albert Schweitzer

Introduction

First light was still an hour away as I awoke in my sleeping bag to the sound of gnawing just outside my tent. Twice I had dismissed this sound and rolled back over for a few more minutes in the comfort of my warm and cozy sleeping bag. It was late September in the Canadian Rockies and for ten days I had hiked the ridges to the sounds of bugling elk, crying loons, and honking Canada geese on their way south. Bighorn sheep and mountain goats had visited the mineral licks nearby and overall the weather had been superb. This morning was crisp and after being disturbed a third time by this mysterious gnawing sound, I pulled myself out of bed and slipped into my clothes. The tent flaps were crusted in frost as was the surrounding campsite. Everything had taken on a bluish tint in the dim light of morning but I immediately made out the silhouette of my morning visitor. A young but plump porcupine had decided that the kindling next to my firering was a bit too much to resist and was munching away on the slivers of aspen. Startled by my emergence he began to waddle down the path toward the lake. I was already up and the sight of this comical fellow seemed to be a good way to pass the morning, so I followed. As I stepped through a group of spruce a sound pierced the morning and literally stunned me into a frozen stance. It was the clearest and most eerie sound that I had ever heard and in a moment a chorus of these haunting calls rang through the forest as golden rays of light sent shafts through frosted woodlands. This was my first experience hearing a pack of wolves howl in a truly pristine setting and my emotions ranged from overwhelming joy to a longing to match a sighting with this wonderful sound that I was hearing. It would be three years before this occurred, but my life had truly been affected by this three minute encounter on the shore of a wilderness lake in Alberta.

CHAPTER ONE

Denning with Wolves

Having hiked through the wilds of Canada and Alaska on many separate occasions, I am certain that my presence has often been observed by the elusive wolf. In the past few years I have witnessed the curious stare of the yellow eyes of the wolf and watched as he silently disappeared into the forest. To know that the wolf will continue to thrive in wilderness adds a valuable element to every outdoor experience in "wolf country."

Wolf pups spend nearly two months in and around the densite. The strong legs and big paws will become valuable tools for this young male as he grows and establishes himself with the pack. His early days of play are important as he learns survival techniques of an effective hunter.

A biologist in Alberta once said that while watching a pack of wolves feed on an elk carcass on a remote flat at the base of the Canadian Rockies, this thought came to him, "If those who hate wolves could only watch a pack in the wild, they would see that there is no more natural a mammal on earth than these. They play and chase and acknowledge one another constantly. There is no constant snarling and fighting but a completely relaxed wild pack on its territory where plenty of food exists and nature is balanced." After eating an average of 5-10 pounds of meat per day, an adult wolf must consume large amounts of water to prevent uremic poisoning from the urea in their meat diet. Dens are almost always located close to a source of water.

To stand in temperatures near zero and watch the dominant wolf lead the pack is a lesson in endurance. Wolves seem to love the cold and can tolerate temperatures down to fifty degrees below zero. They have a single molt in late spring after which short coarse hairs eventually cover their body with long, thick, protective coats. A wolf's head is impressive in size with a mouth containing forty-two teeth and a bite pressure of 1500 pounds per square inch.

Wolves often use the same densite year after year. Most dens are located on a promontory where the wolves can have full awareness of all that moves through their territory. The female goes into her mating cycle in late winter and generally produces four to seven pups in late April or early May. Much of the pack's activity will involve the area near the den. Wolves usually mate for life and bonds are very strong. The father of the pups will bring food to the female while she is nursing the pups. If something should happen to the female while raising the pups, it is very common for another female to take the responsibility of raising them. Pup mortality the first year is greater than 50%, resulting from disease, injuries, and predation.

Wolf pups weigh only one pound at birth and have a *smoky-blue* coat. Their ears are folded and it will take about six weeks for them to become completely perked up. Though the pups can hear in only a few days, it takes 11-15 days before they open their eyes. The pups receive care from the entire pack though the parents are especially attentive.

Pups are weaned at six to eight weeks of age but come out of the den at three to four weeks. Life centers around the den area until a "ground nest" is established. The pack will assist, not only in feeding, but in training and protecting the young pups.

CHAPTER TWO

Caribou and Wolves

On several occasions I have spent time above the Arctic Circle in the area of Bathurst Inlet in the Northwest Territories. The Inuit people are warm and eager to share information regarding the natural history of their homeland. It was here that I gained great insight on the matter of wolves and their involvement with the caribou migration. In the spring the Inuit people leave their village and travel with the caribou. They set up their skin tents and estimate the route of the passing caribou. In days gone by, the hunter would crouch in a ring of rock (known as a hide) and cover himself with a caribou hide until the caribou came close enough to take with his spear. Every part of the caribou was used right down to the sinew that made great rope and tent guy lines and drawcords for winter parkas. There was no waste. The wolf, too, left his territory to follow the caribou. A mammal of great endurance, the wolf can travel 25 to 30 miles in a night. Except for the launch of the attack, the Inuits observed the wolf and caribou as being very calm around each other. Once the kill was made, the pack would remain with the carcass until it was completely consumed. There is no waste in nature.

When early Inuit hunters miscalculated the migration of the caribou, many in the family could perish from hunger. Though the caribou presents an opportunity for the wolf, it is not a given source of food. A healthy adult caribou can out run a wolf easily and in a confrontation a wolf can be fatally injured by the quick hooves and powerful legs of the caribou. The pack will take the weak, the injured, and the vulnerable. The Inuit, as did most Native American people, have great respect for the wolf and observe the wolf at his strongest and at the peak of his sharp intelligence in an effort to provide and survive in a very unforgiving part of the world. The kinship that native people feel toward the wolf is evident in ceremony and in artifacts from the brotherhood between ancient man and wolf.

To be an observer as a pack of wolves organize a hunt is probably one of the greatest marvels in all the world of nature. Consider first that a wolf can pick up the scent of his prey more than 300 yards downwind. Through body language and eye contact, the pack begins to spread out even up to a half mile apart. Slowly and methodically, the escape routes of the prey are cut off. The wolves may sit looking back and forth at each other for the signal that the alpha wolf most likely will initiate. A very organized maneuver closes in on the prey often with positive results.

CHAPTER THREE

Return of the Red Wolf

In the Great Smoky Mountains of Tennessee, an effort is underway to reintroduce the red wolf. In this "island of wildness" comprised of 550,000 acres, lies some ideal habitat for the red wolf. Two pair were brought in to the Smokies from other captive breeding programs. On the morning that I arrived in the containment area I was surprised at the elusive nature of the wolves, given that they had been exposed to humans most of their lives. As I remained alone in the compound to try and photograph these soon-to-be historic mammals, the pair began to circle the perimeter of the enclosure. On several occasions the male crossed diagonally in front of me as if to test my intentions. The size of their paws and the length of their legs impressed me greatly as he thundered by repeatedly. It is too soon to predict an outcome for this attempt at establishing a wolf population, but the ingredients are here for a genuine effort.

Eastern deciduous woodlands provide small game, abundant water, and plenty of shelter for the red wolf introduction program.

After weeks of great expectations, I revisited the red wolf compound located in a shady mountain cove of the Smoky Mountains. Four pups were born and doing well. Their character and "wild" behavior spelled hope for the program. It would be a year later that we tunneled through 30 feet of hay in a deserted barn to find a second litter born in the park. Possibly the only way to truly give the wolves a chance to claim this area as their new home will be to let them roam and multiply freely. The latest methods of tracking and research are being applied here as the reintroduction is being scrutinized by an assortment of interested parties nationwide.

CHAPTER FOUR

Wolf Ways

It was at this location in Kootenay Provincial Park, Alberta, that I first encountered a pack of wolves. The peaceful setting of wilderness became a perfect backdrop for all that one would expect to be included in a wolf's habitat. The morning was heavily frosted and foggy and the sun had not reached the level seen above. The shadows were deep and the loon had not begun to cry, yet all the woodland creatures realized the presence of "wild hunters." I heard the gentle crunch of footsteps on the brittle, frozen grasses but not until the first wail echoed through the morning stillness did I realize what an eventful morning this would be. The long mournful howl was cut off by two to three matching howls and higher pitched shorter howls ensued. The shadows never gave up the detail of the pack as they continued their chorus on the ridgeline, but it was as if I had been given a private concert that would affect me for the rest of my life.

As I travel throughout natural areas around our country, I sense that increasing numbers of people are coming to understand the vital role of predators in the scheme of nature's balance. This awareness may be the best chance for survival that the wolves have.

With great passion and insight for all living things, Albert Schweitzer stated early in the century, "The friend of nature is the man who feels himself inwardly united with everything that lives in nature, who shares in the fate of all creatures, helps them when he can in their pain and need, and as far as possible avoids injuring or taking life."

As I walked across this meadow in the high country of the Bridger Mountains in Montana, I realized what excellent habitat exists here for the wolf. Though little sign would indicate that the wolf still lingers here, elk, deer, and sheep thrive in a secluded and natural area. Between 1883 and 1918, over 80,000 wolves were poisoned, shot, or trapped under a bounty system in the state of Montana.

Throughout my days of observing the wolf, it would seem to me that water is no barrier to this determined animal. From the crossing of frozen lakes in winter to the splashing through icy streams in spring, the wolf takes the shortest distance between two points when hunting. During the warm summer months, water is a sure relief from the heat and on occasion the pack seems to intentionally splash through shallow rivers and creeks. It has been noted that most prey animals will gain the advantage of escape after reaching a depth of three feet but other observations note seeing a wolf take a deer while swimming along side of it during the chase and one account recorded seeing a wolf treading water while feeding on a moose carcass in the river.

Many times I have searched for the wolves near their densite only to detect a single wolf bedded in the grasses only a few yards from the opening.

Wolves have been recorded running more than 25 miles per hour over a period of up to 20 minutes. This extremely strenuous period most always requires the wolf to lie down to recuperate. The exhaustion and overheating is controlled by panting and a short period of inactivity.

The social organization of the wolf pack sets the wolf apart from the rest of the animal world. The pack may consist of four to seven parents, their young and close relatives all following a very strict hierarchy. The number of wolves in a pack can vary from four to twenty or more but a common number within a pack is six to fifteen wolves. The numbers and availability and type of prey within the wolf pack's territory strongly affects the size of the pack. The pack seems to be held together by the strong bonds of affection. These bonds closely resemble the relationship between a dog and his human companion in the way that the wolf reacts and relates to its fellow pack members. Every wolf is aware of his or her role through the strict hierarchy that is established. The roles are constantly reinforced through acts of threats (growls, snarls, teeth-baring, etc.), submissive postures, and affectionate responses like licking and mouth nuzzling.

The alpha male controls the activity of the pack. On several occasions I have witnessed squabbles break out in the pack but most were near the mating cycle in late winter. Threats rarely turn to outright fighting. Posturing and facial expression convey a very clear message and response. The common sight in true wilderness is to observe a contented pack of wolves working and living together in harmony with each member accepting and carrying out his or her role within the organization.

In my many years of observing and photographing wild animals, I have found very few situations where I felt even remotely threatened. I'm sure that there are several reasons for feeling this way and often it comes down to a simple matter of mutual respect and understanding behavior. If there is one mammal that perhaps deserves to be resentful of intrusion, it quite possibly is the female moose. I would certainly give her a great right of way when encountered in the backcountry. For sixteen years I have spent time in Denali National Park of Alaska. After the cow moose successfully drops her calf in the spring, she may likely have twins in following years. Estimates are, in this area, that of the sets of twins born to moose in the spring, only one pair in fifteen will survive to fall because of predation by grizzlies and wolves. The cow can easily defend one of her calves against an attack but when separated from the cow and first calf, the second is very vulnerable and often taken. Therefore, it would stand to reason that a cow moose would be very defensive toward any foreign interference in her area. Wolves can locate their prey in one of three ways: scent location (as mentioned, a wolf can pick up the scent of the moose as far as 300 yards downwind), chance (hunting packs often run up on prey when covering their territory), and by tracking their prey by means of sight, scent, and hearing.

It was an exciting event the first time I watched a red fox leap up in the air and pounce upon a field mouse. Equally impressive was the day I watched a peregrine falcon go through its maneuvers to take a jay from midair. The hunt in nature can only be appreciated when we consider that nature is not based on what we feel is "fair or humane" but on what it takes to survive. An effective predator such as the wolf will cull the sick or the weak though he is an opportunist and will take whatever prey presents itself. The fact is that in many cases the predator strengthens the prey species and often encourages productivity in the herd. It definitely controls numbers in populations of prey. It has always been gratifying for me to note that there is no place in nature for the lazy, the worthless, nor the unmotivated.

CHAPTER FIVE

Wolf Talk

Across North America outdoor enthusiasts are being lured to wolf habitat to experience the "call of the wild." In Algonquin Park, wolf howls are a common activity as they are at the International Wolf Headquarters in Ely, Minnesota. As these avenues of education draw us closer to appreciating the uniqueness of the wolf, it is equally important to note the reasons why wolves do howl.

Wolf howls have added a great amount of depth to many of my outdoor experiences over the past few years. More often than not, I have only heard, (lacking the sighting of the pack) not knowing exactly what function the howl performed.

It has often been said that on occasion the wolves howl just for the joy of it but mostly the vocalization is far more involved. Stray members of the pack may be called to identify themselves and regroup. Wolves of other packs may be put on notice that they have entered another pack's territory and stand to be in danger. These vocalizations may prevent direct encounter with other pack members and thus prevent injury or worse. On the occasion of making a kill, the wolves often howl to alert pack members lagging behind or separated due to the maneuver of the hunt.

It seems that wolves will howl from most any posture. On several occasions I have witnessed wolves howling while lying down and sitting and on one occasion I watched a wolf scent his territory while howling.

Howls have been only a part of the vocalizations that I have witnessed within the wolf pack. Whimpers, growls, moans, groans, and yelps all have proven to be significant in showing the wolves' response to fear, pleasure, and even pain. It would appear that many times a howling session is an inspirational time to prepare for a hunt or a day of travel across the territory. The idea of an "audible fence" around the pack's territory is a great indication of the wolf's ability to coexist with other packs and prevent overlapping. Most prey species seem to be unaffected for the most part by the howling of the pack.

Often food fights become a bluff to test the hierarchy within the pack. An alpha male may fight with several adults and after chasing them away he could easily give up his position to a young pack member. I watched as a young male darted in on a kill to grab an elk leg and race back into the woods. For several minutes he was chased by other wolves as the game continued. The severity of the game may be communicated by the positioning of the tail. A tail held high indicates dominance while a tucked tail signals a submissive posture.

The alpha wolf expresses his dominance by baring his teeth, slightly opening the mouth, and wrinkling the skin on his forehead. These signs of communication are accompanied by a still tail rather than a wagging one, by flattened ears rather than erect, and by bristled hair rather than flattened. All these signs appear according to the mood that is provoked during encounters with other wolves. Verbally, there is a growl meaning a direct threat.

The act of fraternizing among wolves is a very friendly occasion. A good example occurs before their departure for a hunt. The wolves have often been observed wagging tails in a tight group, eventually sitting at which point a chorus of howls breaks out.

On occasion, I have spotted a single wolf without any sign of other pack members in the area. While it is not unusual for a wolf to wander far from the group on a hunt, there is the occasional "lone wolf" situation. Many factors can contribute to a wolf's status as being alone. When prey species numbers crash drastically, a pack may simply disband for the survival of each member. Other factors involve an imbalance in the hierarchy that makes up the pack, thus forcing younger males to be expelled from the pack. A lone wolf seldom howls or makes scent markings. He will travel in "safe zones" between neighboring wolf pack territories. He will constantly search for a partner and a territory which is his true nature.

Often during play, females will bite at the neck of the male wolf. When I first observed this behavior, I was sure that this was somewhat of a painful experience, but, after examining the winter pelt of a wolf, I found it near impossible to force my finger through the thick hair to the actual hide. The thickness and warmth of the fur allows the wolf to sleep in a circled position in minus 40 degrees temperatures and in total comfort.

In late November I often return to the Chilkat Valley near Haines, Alaska to observe and photograph the thousands of bald eagles that gather there. My greatest joy within this experience is to get up before daylight and walk down by the Chilkat River where the leads in the river remain open and the cottonwoods overhang the shoreline. Here the eagles roost overhead by the hundreds waiting for the warmth of morning sun and the opportunity to retrieve the spawned out salmon.

In 1989, just before Thanksgiving, I was on the Chilkat. It was just before daylight and I walked in knee deep snow past a fallen cabin and on through the woods to the river. A muffled rumble like rolling rocks in water caught my attention; as I looked to my left, I saw two very beautiful and healthy wolves romping in the snow. We saw each other at the same time and exchanged glances. It seemed like a long time but I'm sure it was only seconds as the wolves proceeded in the same playful manner that they had appeared. This was their home. They are forest dwellers here and stable in this healthy range.

CHAPTER SIX

Where Wolves Roam

Where elk and wolves overlap, the wolf will often be blamed for making a kill when actually it was a coyote. If a wolf can catch a coyote in his territory he will kill him and he will pursue a coyote with all the strength and agility he possesses. It will be very interesting to watch upcoming developments in the greater Yellowstone ecosystem as the numbers of wolves grow and establish territories. The coyote population will surely be affected as well as keeping the elk population healthy and in check.

The wolf is primarily a hunter of big game. He can literally smell his prey a mile away. His endurance is greater than that of the mighty grizzlies and the cunning mountain lion, therefore making him a more effective hunter. This is especially true when considering the multiplied effectiveness of the pack. His strength allows him to cover up to 125 miles in a twenty-four-hour period.

Grant Pearson was one of the first park rangers in what was then Mt. McKinley National Park. He climbed the 20,320 foot summit when means were crude. He lived in the bush and enforced wildlife laws in a *"rough and tumble"* era. In his book, *My Life of High Adventure*, he writes of his rugged wilderness experiences. He observed the wolf during hunts and lived with the wolf daily. He once wrote around 1940, "Wild animals are not supposed to be as heavily endowed with principles as men are; but I never heard of a wild animal yet that tried to do a really mean, low-down thing. I guess it's because they've got no room in their skulls for easy rationalizing." This tongue-in-cheek statement surely gives credence to the wolves' behavior.

Wolves can spend literally hours searching out small mammals such as this arctic ground squirrel. Their approach includes stalking and pouncing on their target. I have observed a wolf missing his potential victim then marking the ground, scratching the spot, and rolling in this spot for a lengthy period. These small critters are a small but often worthwhile meal.

By spring the temperatures have warmed up enough to affect the wolf's daily behavior. He will cool off by panting though he also possesses sweat glands in the pads of his paws and on the skin surface. The secretion of sweat performs functions beyond cooling, however. It rids the body of wastes and even allows the wolf recognition by scent among the other wolves. Sweat in fur-bearing animals also suggests alarm or aggression.

This little fellow's mother began preparation for him long before he entered into the world. She dug out her den possibly three to four weeks before the pups were born. She only comes into her mating cycle one time per year and will not produce another litter of pups that year.

Denali National Park is still one of the very best areas in North America to view wolves. Though it is not a guarantee, in sixteen years of travel I have seen wolves almost every time and some years on multiple occasions. Denali is over five and one half million acres. Alaska in general is one of the last strongholds for the wolf in the fifty states. Eighty-five percent of the 586,000 square miles is considered wolf habitat. In some areas wolf densities are estimated at one wolf per 25 square miles. Prey densities, diseases, and harvest have affected their numbers in recent years.

The female wolf will spend only short periods of time in the sun during spring and summer. Wolves are very sensitive to heat and are more often found in shaded areas during the day. The night will be reserved for hunting.

The entire focus of the pack changes when pups are born. The pack is constantly there to play with them, protect them, educate them, and feed them.

Wolves are known for leaving "scent posts" or simply scent markings throughout their territory. They are to the nose what howls are to the ear. They identify the territory and warn other packs to beware; they identify the wolf that left the mark by age and sex. It is somewhat of a signature. The scent posts develop a map that aids in finding hunting routes through the territory and in returning home after maneuvers of any type. They lead to kill sites and allow pack members to come and go in silence when necessary.

When European settlers arrived in North America, wolves occupied nearly the whole continent with the exception of areas in the Southeast coastal plains and a couple of areas in Baja and central Mexico. It is such a concern to those who enjoy the outdoors to develop an understanding of the flora and fauna that make up the natural areas left for us to enjoy. Henry David Thoreau said in his journals, "I seek acquaintance with Nature—to know her moods and manners. Primitive nature is the most interesting to me..."

In winter the pack roams freely. The pads of their feet are in constant contact with ice and snow. I have often watched a wolf lick and bite at crusted ice between the pads of the paw. Nature has provided very perfectly for the insulation of the wolf. This prolonged contact activates a special regulatory adaption: the foot pad temperature adjusts to just above the freezing point for the tissue and is regulated independently of the rest of the wolf's body. The wolf, in this way, experiences no unnecessary loss of body heat.

Even in play fights and quarrels between pack members, seldom can one wolf bring harm to the other. Their winter coat is two-and one-half inches thick and made up of tight layers of warm hair and even longer guard hairs that often collect a thin layer of snow and provide further insulation.

The wolf has been maligned as a vicious predator far too long. Never in history has there been a documented case of a healthy, wild wolf attacking a human being in North America. As far back as 1634, William Wood wrote in *Of the Beasts that Live on the Land*, "It is never known yet that a wolf ever set upon a man or woman."

CHAPTER SEVEN

A Last Stronghold

It was autumn in Alaska, which is generally the last week in August and the first week in September. I had just finished one of the most wonderful weeks of all my fifteen years of adventure travel into Denali National Park. I had arrived on September 3rd with a group of folks from around the country who had signed up to go with me to Camp Denali, a wilderness lodge ninety miles inside the park. It snowed throughout the night with around eight inches on the ground. The birch, aspen, alder, and willow were in full glory of color, slightly adorned with new fallen snow. The journey from Anchorage to Denali took around five hours. At the train station we had reloaded our gear onto buses bound for the lodge.

At this point the experience takes on a feel of awe and wonder because Denali is restricted to a select few vehicles to preserve the habitat and behavior of the mammals there. For this reason alone every turn in the road presents a potential exhibit of North America's wildness. Usually we begin seeing moose around the kettle ponds followed by an explosion of wings as a covey of willow ptarmigan take flight across the tundra. Northern harriers and golden eagles are commonplace across the rolling tundra and high on the ridges. Dall sheep are soon spotted on gentle slopes or rugged outcroppings. Within a couple of hours we enter some of the best grizzly habitat in the park and seldom are we without a sighting of a male digging out ground squirrels or a female grizzly taking her cubs through a blueberry field. As far as the eye can see a carpet of red, yellow, and orange stretches to the foothills of the Alaska range which arches 150 miles through the heart of Denali. Our minds are not expectant of a wolf sighting. It is so rare in other parts of North America that most of the group have focused their expectations on other mammals.

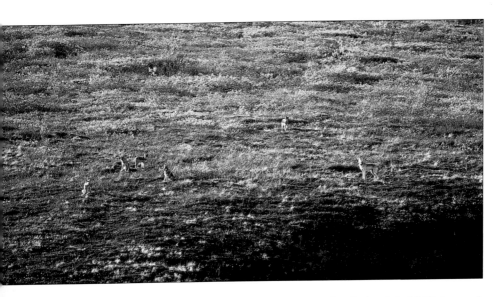

We arrived at camp around dusk. Located along a ridge facing Mt. McKinley and looking across Wonder Lake, the grouping of cabins are thoughtfully arranged to allow each of us to have a true Alaskan experience. The interpretation will give each person a depth of natural history information ranging from glaciers to permafrost to gyrfalcons and wolverines. We could not have been prepared for what was to come. The weather broke that evening with a wash of pink alpenglow that could have signaled the opening of the heavens. We were up throughout the night watching the swirls of northern lights. The next few days were filled with once-in-a-lifetime experiences of hikes on the glacier with a wolverine shadowing the group on an opposite ridge. A sow with cubs dug for ground squirrels just across the way and later slept with her cubs on her back. Moose and caribou sparred near the ponds where beaver were towing willow branches to store for the winter. The best was yet to come.

On September 11th we were up at 5 AM and loaded for the long trip back to the train station shortly thereafter. The morning was beginning to break with shafts of light striking the east face of "the Great One." After a ways, I spotted a couple of adult wolves hunting in a drainage about 60 yards out. I asked the group to be very still and quiet. The wolves moved up on a flat above the drainage. They were joined by two more adults and five pups. We watched as the lead wolves canvassed the area. After several minutes the lead wolf stopped, lifted his head, and began to howl. The adult wolves joined in and then the pups began. The chorus of untamed music must have lasted five to ten minutes as golden light covered the pack with morning beauty. Nothing would top this; we had truly witnessed one of the greatest events in all of wilderness.

A bull moose on the tundra is not a consideration for wolves unless the moose is injured or showing signs of fatigue. The exception would be in times of low prey density at which time the pack would work the moose to a point of fleeing and through constant pursuit the pack might eventually overcome him. When a kill is made, often meat is stored in the stomach and taken back to the pups where it is presented again as food. The nose of the moose is his number one prey finder with the ears following a close second. The ability of the wolf to distinguish the difference in tones is so acute that he can identify a vole traveling beneath the surface of the snow.

The year of the wolf is broken into two major categories: April to late fall is spent near the densite building, strengthening, and reinforcing the bonds within the pack while raising new members of the "family." In October the pack moves together to freely roam through the winter in search of food. Their intelligence has given them the ability to deal with changing circumstances from year to year.

While the wolf can maintain a trotting speed of five miles per hour throughout the day, he can surge at speeds up to forty miles per hour and maintain twenty mile per hour chases for fifteen to twenty minutes.

The plight of the wolf is uncertain. The key to survival is understanding. The ability to understand may surely come when each of us shed the fears and preconceived ideas that we have been taught in relation to "wildness." When we take time to ponder the thought of beauty we hopefully will realize that beauty comes as a result of balance and balance is predetermined. We are surely guardians of a world that is changing rapidly and swallowing up wilderness at an unforgivable pace. John Muir says, "Go into the mountains and get their good tidings..." The man or woman who spends time alone in the outdoors will find answers and sense a responsibility for those who cannot speak for themselves.

"Have you ever stood where the silences brood
And vast horizons begin,
at the dawn of the day to behold far away
The goal you would strive for and win?"

from "The Land Beyond" by Robert Service